Theo Walcott

by

Andy Croft

Illustrated by Dylan Gibson

First published in 2012 in Great Britain by
Barrington Stoke Ltd
18 Walker St, Edinburgh, EH3 7LP

www.barringtonstoke.co.uk

ISBN: 978-1-84299-484-9

Printed in China by Leo

Contents

Chapter 1
Germany 2006

It's the Summer of 2006.

England are getting ready for the World Cup finals in Germany. The fans can't wait. They think that England can win the World Cup this time. The England Manager Sven-Göran Eriksson has some great players, like

Steven Gerrard, Michael Owen, Frank Lampard, Ashley Cole, John Terry, Wayne Rooney and David Beckham.

But the strikers Wayne Rooney and Michael Owen are not fully fit. Eriksson needs to take another striker. Most people think he will take Darren Bent from Charlton or Jermain Defoe from Spurs. Some people think he should take Andy Johnson from Crystal Palace or Dean Ashton from West Ham.

But Eriksson picks a young striker who has never played for England before. He hasn't even played in the Premier League. He has only scored six goals in his career. And he is only 17 years old.

His name is Theo Walcott. Not many people have heard of him. Not many people have ever seen him play. Not many people think he should be in the England team. But Eriksson thinks he is ready for the World Cup.

The World Cup doesn't go well. England are knocked out in the quarter-finals again. On penalties, again. And Theo Walcott never kicks a ball. He never even plays.

The fans are gutted. Most people blame Eriksson. But some fans blame Theo Walcott. They say he shouldn't have gone. They say he is too young. They say he is not good enough to play for England.

After all, who is Theo Walcott?

Chapter 2

T.J.

Theo James Walcott was born in Stanmore in London, on 16 March 1989. His dad worked for the RAF. His mum was a nurse. Theo grew up in the small village of Compton in Berkshire with his mum and dad, his brother Ashley and his sister Hollie. He went to the local primary school and then to

the Downs School. Theo liked school. He was
popular. Everyone called him "T.J.".

His best subjects were Maths and Art.
One of his paintings was so good that the
head-teacher hung it on the wall. It's still
there today. He also liked Drama, and acting
in school plays. He once starred in *Bugsy
Malone*.

Best of all, Theo liked sport. He was a
very fast runner. He broke the school
records for running 100m and 200m. When
he was 14, he ran 100m in just 11.5 seconds!

He was one of fastest cross-country runners in the whole county.

And of course Theo liked football. He supported Liverpool, like his dad. He played for Compton Primary School and for the District Primary Schools team. He also played for AFC Newbury. In his first game for Newbury he scored 6 goals. He scored 100 goals in one season. He once scored nine goals in one game – a triple hat-trick. Theo was so fast that the fans called him the "Newbury Express".

When Theo was ten, he was so good that he was picked for special coaching. The coaching was at the Centre of Excellence in Swindon Town. Soon the big clubs began to hear about the fast kid from Swindon. Chelsea and Southampton sent scouts to watch him. Chelsea invited him to be a ball-boy at Stamford Bridge. They hoped that Theo would sign for them. But that day Chelsea were playing Liverpool and that's why Theo went. He just wanted to meet Michael Owen and Robbie Fowler! He even had his photo taken with Michael Owen.

Theo's mum was a Southampton fan. In those days, Southampton were in the Premier League. Theo went to look round the Dell – the Southampton ground. He really liked it. Southampton seemed a friendly club. And it wasn't very far away from Theo's home.

So Theo joined the Southampton Academy. Southampton paid Swindon £2,000 for him. He was still only 12. He was so happy he jumped up and down on his bed. He jumped so hard he broke it!

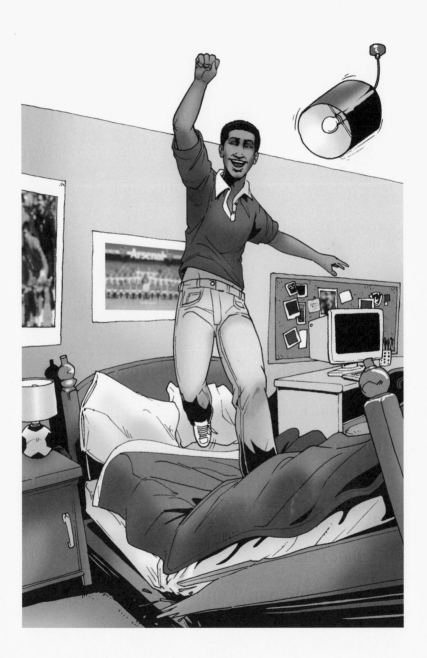

Chapter 3

Saints

Theo had to train hard as a Youth player at Southampton. He had to pick up balls and cones and bibs when first-team training was over. And he had to take all the dirty kit to get washed.

But Theo soon made a name for himself at the club. The manager Harry Redknapp couldn't believe how fast he was. "The kid can run through puddles and not make a splash," Harry said.

In September 2004, Theo became the youngest player ever to play for Southampton's reserve team. He was also the star of the Southampton Youth side when it reached the final of the FA Youth Cup in 2005. Gareth Bale was also in the team. He plays for Spurs now.

Theo was still in the Reserves when Southampton were relegated at the end of 2005. George Burley took Harry Redknapp's place as manager. George asked Theo to come with the first team on a pre-season tour of Scotland. Theo had only just left school.

In August 2005, Theo came on as a sub in a 0–0 draw with Wolves. This made him the youngest ever player to play for the Southampton first team. He was 16 years and 143 days old.

Theo came on at the start of a game for the first time against Leeds in October 2005. He scored his first goal. He scored again a few days later in an away game against Milwall. And then again on his full home debut against Stoke.

In two seasons, Theo played 55 games and scored six goals for Southampton. But Southampton needed money. The manager George Burley had to think about selling his best players, like Kenwyne Jones, Gareth Bale – and Theo Walcott.

By now several Premier League clubs wanted to buy Theo. Chelsea said they would give Southampton £15 million for him. But Theo wanted to go to Arsenal, to play with Thierry Henry.

Theo went to Arsenal in January 2006 for £5 million. It was a record fee for a teenager. And Theo was still only 16.

Chapter 4

Gunners

The Arsenal manager Arsène Wenger gave Theo the number 32 shirt. This was the same shirt Theo wore at Southampton. He soon made a name for himself at his new club. The other players called him "Tiger", because they thought he looked like the golfer Tiger Woods. But also he was as fast as a tiger. And deadly with a ball.

When Theo started training everyone saw that he was great. He could play on the left or on the right. He could cross or cut inside. He could dribble or sprint to the line. He had a fantastic shot. And most of all, Theo was fast. He was even faster than Thierry Henry. He was the fastest player at the club. He could run 40 metres in five seconds. He once ran 100 metres in 10.3 seconds. The world-record is 9.5 seconds.

Theo played his first Premier League game for Arsenal on 19 August 2006. This was the first day of the new season, and he came on as a sub against Aston Villa. He set up a goal for Gilberto Silva.

The next month he played his first Champions' League game against Dinamo Zagreb. The ref gave him a yellow card because he took a shot after the ref had blown for offside. But in the last minute of the game he set up a goal for Flamini.

Theo was the youngest Arsenal player ever to play in Europe.

Theo played his first league game at home against Watford on 14 October 2006. He scored his first goal for Arsenal in the 2007 League Cup Final against Chelsea. He scored his first Champions League goal against Slavia Prague. He came off the bench in a game against Liverpool and ran past four defenders to set up a goal for Adebayor.

At the end of 2007–8 Theo had scored seven goals in 20 games.

That Summer Thierry Henry left Arsenal for Barcelona. Wenger gave Henry's number 14 shirt to Theo. The fans called him "the new Thierry Henry".

Theo started the next season as a regular member of the first team. Sometimes he played in right midfield. Sometimes he played as a winger. But in November he hurt his right shoulder while training with England. He was out of action for five months.

Theo was back in the team by April 2009. He seemed sharper and faster than ever. He scored a great shot from the edge of the box with his left foot in a game against Burnley. He scored a fantastic goal against Barcelona in the Champions' League. Then he set up Nicklas Bendtner to score in the second leg.

Barcelona star Lionel Messi was amazed by Theo's speed. "He is one of the most dangerous players I have ever played against," Lionel said. The Barcelona manager said that Theo was so fast, "you need a gun to stop him"!

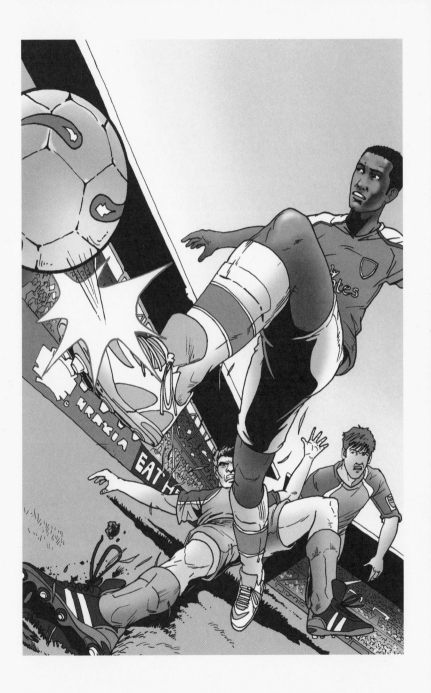

Now everyone was talking about Theo Walcott.

Chapter 5

England

By the time Theo was 17, he had played for England under-16s, under-17s and under-19s. Then on 25 May 2006, Eriksson put him on the bench for an England B team game against Belarus. When Theo came on as a sub in the second half, he was the youngest player ever to play for the England B team.

Five days later, Theo became the youngest player ever to win a full England cap. It was in a friendly against Hungary at Old Trafford. He was just 17 years and 75 days old. His speed and skill helped England win 3–1.

After the 2006 World Cup, Steve McClaren took Eriksson's place as England manager. McClaren didn't think Theo was ready for the England team. So Theo started playing for England Under-21s. He won his first cap against Moldova in 2006. He also scored two

goals. This made him the youngest player ever to score for the "Young Lions".

Two months later Theo scored two goals against Germany to send England into the under-21 European Championships.

In the Summer of 2009, Theo helped the England under-21s reach the Under-21s European Championship Final. In 15 games, Theo scored six goals for the team.

Around this time, England had another new manager. He was called Fabio Capello and he liked the look of Theo so he put him back in the first team. Theo came on as sub in a 3–0 win in a friendly against Trinidad and Tobago.

Theo was Fabio Capello's first-choice winger as the England team fought to get to the World Cup finals. He played in six of England's ten group games. He helped beat Belarus, Andorra (twice) and Kazakhstan (twice). He scored a fantastic hat-trick against Croatia. Theo is the youngest player ever to score a hat-trick for England. England won nine games, lost only one and came out top of their group. They scored 34 goals and only let in six.

Theo's hat-trick helped England reach the World Cup finals in South Africa. This time everyone thought he would be in the World Cup team. But Capello didn't pick him. This time no one could believe it!

Without Theo Walcott, England just couldn't score goals. They looked slow compared to the other teams. The World Cup went badly again. England drew with the USA and then with Algeria. They beat

Slovenia, but then they were knocked out by Germany in the quarter-finals. Again.

England fans were gutted again. But this time no one blamed Theo Walcott.

Chapter 6
Beautiful Football

Arsenal manager Arsène Wenger believes in beautiful football. He likes players who are fast and skilful – like Fabregas, Eduardo, Nasri, Arshavin, Ramsey, Rosicky, Wilshere and Theo Walcott.

At the start of the 2010–11 season, Theo scored his first Premier League hat-trick as Arsenal beat Blackpool 6–0. He scored once against Blackburn Rovers and twice against Newcastle United. By the end of October, Theo had scored a goal for every 48 minutes he was on the pitch.

But then in February he twisted his leg in a game against Stoke. This meant he missed the League Cup Final and a Champions' League game against Barcelona. He was back for the last game of the season, when he came off the bench to score against Fulham.

It was his best season yet for Arsenal, with 13 goals in 25 games.

In his first five seasons at Arsenal, Theo had played 100 games and scored 31 goals. That's one goal every three games. Not bad for a winger.

The Gunners played some of the best football in Europe. But they just couldn't win any trophies. They finished 4th and 3rd in the League. They reached the semi-final of the FA Cup. They reached the final of the League Cup in 2007 and 2011. They reached

the semi-finals of the Champions' League.
But they didn't win anything.

Arsène Wenger was frustrated. So were
the Arsenal fans. So were some of the
players. In the summer of 2011 some of
Arsenal's best players left the club. People
even said that Chelsea wanted to buy Theo
Walcott. But Arsène Wenger didn't want to
sell one of his best young players. And Theo
didn't want to leave.

He wanted to stay and win something
with Arsenal.

Chapter 7

Tiger

Today, Theo earns £3 million a year. He has bought a house for his mum, dad and brother near the Arsenal training ground.

His cousin Jacob plays for Reading and England under-17s. His sister Hollie is a body-builder.

Theo has been going out with his girlfriend Melanie since he was 17. She is training to be a physio. He bought her a Ferrari for her 21st birthday. She said it was too flash, so Theo drives it instead. They have a dog called Diesel.

When Theo is not training, he likes playing golf. He likes listening to Jay-Z, Usher, hip-hop and R'n'B. He likes watching *The Fresh Prince of Bel Air* and *Lost* on TV. His all-time favourite film is *King Kong*. He likes karaoke, and the song he likes to sing best is *Ain't No Sunshine When She's Gone*.

Theo doesn't drink, and he doesn't go clubbing. And he doesn't use Twitter.

Theo visits lots of schools for the Football Foundation. He does a lot of work for charities like "Build a School" and "Best Beginnings".

He also likes to read. He was going to be in the film *Harry Potter and the Order of the Phoenix*, but he had to drop out because of training. (Mel has a speaking part in *Harry Potter and the Half-Blood Prince*.)

Theo has even written a series of books for kids about an ace young footballer called "T.J." who is very fast. They are called *T.J. and the Hat-trick*, *T.J. and the Cup Run*, *T.J. and the Penalty* and *T.J. and the Winning Goal*. They're really good.

Theo Walcott is famous all over the world now. He has been voted BBC Young Sports Personality of the Year. In 2008 he helped to carry the Olympic Flame through London on its way to China.

Now everyone has heard of Theo Walcott.

Our books are tested
for children and young people by
children and young people.

Thanks to everyone who consulted on
a manuscript for their time and effort in
helping us to make our books better
for our readers.

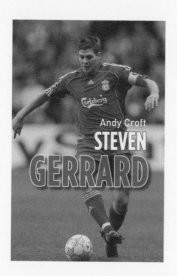

Steven Gerrard
by
Andy Croft

School boy footballer.
Liverpool champion.
England Captain.
How did Stevie G. get to
the top?
Find out here!

Amir Khan
by
Andy Croft

School boy boxer.
Silver medal at the
Olympics.
World champion.
How did the boy from
Bolton become such a
superstar?
Find out here!

Lewis Hamilton
by
Andy Croft

Lewis Hamilton is the first ever black Formula 1 champion.
How did he get from go-karts to global fame?
Find out here!

Sol Campbell
by
Andy Croft

From racism to success.
From hard times to fast cars.
From school team to World Cup squad.
The true story of fame, fortune and a footballing superstar.

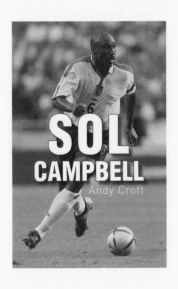

You can order these books directly from our website at
www.barringtonstoke.co.uk